Polish

Christmas

Cookbook

© Copyright 2017. Laura Sommers.
All rights reserved.
No part of this book may be reproduced in any form or by any electronic or mechanical means without written permission of the author. All text, illustrations and design are the exclusive property of
Laura Sommers

Introduction 1

Polish Mushroom Soup - Zupa Grzybowa 2

Barszcz - Polish Beet Soup 3

Uszka - Polish Mushroom Dumplings 4

Fish in Aspic - Ryba w Galarecie 6

Polish Rolled Herring - Rolmops 7

Polish Pike - Szczupak po Polsku..................................8

Sauerkraut with Mushrooms - Kapusta z Grzybami........9

Noodles with Cabbage - Kluski z kapusta.....................10

Mushroom Cabbage Rolls - Golabki z Grzybami...........11

Polish Dumplings - Pierogi...13

Sauerkraut and Mushroom Filling 15

Potato and Cheese Filling..16

Noodles with Poppy Seeds - Kluski z Makiem...............17

Dried Fruit Compote - Kompot z Owocow Suszonych ..18

Christmas Wheat Berry Pudding - Kutia 19

Polish Almond Soup - Zupa migdalowa 20

Polish Honey Spice Cookies - Pierniczki 21

Polish Kolaczki Cookies - Kolaczki 23

Polish Dried Mushroom Soup - Zupa Grzybowa 24

Polish Pickle Soup - Zupa Ogórkowa 26

Polish Potato Soup - Zupa Ziemniaczana 27

Polish Tomato-Rice Soup - Zupa Pomidorowa Ryzu 28

Polish Barley Soup - Krupnik 29

Polish Split Pea Soup - Zupa Grochowka 30

Polish Beets with Sour Cream - Buraczki ze Smietana .31

Polish Cucumbers in Sour Cream 32

Polish Creamed Beet Barszcz Soup - Barszcz Zabielany 33

Polish Light Rye Bread with Caraway Seeds..................34

Split Peas and Cabbage - Kapusta z Grochem...............36

Polish Sweet-Sour Red Cabbage - Czerwona Kapusta Zasmażana 38

Sausage and Noodle Casserole 39

Polish Cabbage Potato Casserole 40

Polish Haluski - Noodles, Onion and Cabbage...............41

Polish Sausage Casserole 42

Polish Nalesniki 43

Polish Sweet Bread 44

Polish Sourdough Rye Bread..46

Polish Cream Cheese Coffee Cake 48

Polish Noodles and Cottage Cheese 50

Polish Galicyjskie Cookies 51

Polish Christmas Cookies 52

Sweet Polish Cherry Cake 53

Polish Yeast Plum Cake - Drozdzowka.......................... 54

Polish Apple Pancakes - Racuchy z Jablkami................56

Polish Stuffed Cabbage 57
Bigos - Polish Hunter's Stew 58
Chlodnik - Cold Polish Beet Soup 60
Polish Chili 61
Polish Rice Cake 62
Polish Jam Crescents - Rogaliki 63
Polish Babka Cake 65
Polish Stewed Cabbage 67
Polish Perogies 68
About the Author 70
Other Books by Laura Sommers 71

Introduction

Christmas Eve is called Wigilia in Poland, held on December 24th. It encompasses the entire day, includes Christmas Eve feast and then extends to the midnight mass held at the Roman Catholic Church.

This Christmas Eve feast is often called wieczerza or wieczerza wigilijna which means "dinner" or "large supper." Around dusk of Christmas Eve, children will look for the first star in the sky. The feasting traditionally begins once the First Star has been sighted by children in the sky at dusk (around 5 p.m.) Therefore, Christmas is called "Gwiazdka" which means the little star, referring to the Star of Bethlehem.

Originally, people fasted the entire day before the feast, but that tradition has been abandoned. The feast includes foods from the four corners of the earth and originally did not include meat. Today, meat and fish are a big part of the festivities.

This cookbook contains some of the best loved recipes for the Christmas Eve and Christmas holiday season in Poland.

Polish Mushroom Soup - Zupa Grzybowa

Ingredients:

16 oz. fresh mushrooms (portabella mushrooms preferred)
2 oz. dried mushrooms (optional)
1 large onion
4 tbsps. butter
Juice of 1/2 lemon
1/4 cup water
6 cups rich mushroom, vegetable, or beef broth
1 cup sour cream
3 tbsps. flour
salt and pepper to taste
1/4 cup fresh dill, chopped

Directions:

1. If using dried mushrooms, soak them in hot water for two hours.
2. Drain, squeeze out excess water, and chop finely.
3. Wash and coarsely chop fresh mushrooms.
4. Sauté onions in butter over medium heat for 5-7 minutes until softened, add mushrooms and sauté for another 15 minutes.
5. Add lemon juice and water and cook covered for another an additional 5 minutes.
6. Transfer mushrooms to a soup pot, add the broth, and bring to a low simmer. Blend the sour cream with the flour and mix well.
7. Gradually add 1 cup of the hot soup to the sour cream and mix until smooth.
8. Pour the sour cream mixture slowly to the pot, stirring constantly.
9. Simmer for five minutes, stirring occasionally.
10. Serve garnished with chopped dill.

Barszcz - Polish Beet Soup

Ingredients:

3 or 4 cans of whole beets
2 cans of vegetable, mushroom, or beef broth
2 cups of water
4 cups of tomato or vegetable juice
Juice of 1/2 lemon
1/2 tsp. sugar
1/2 tsp. pepper
1 tsp. salt

Directions:

1. Strain the beets and set aside.
2. Combine beet juice, broth, water and tomato or vegetable juice in an enameled or stainless steel soup pot.
3. Bring to a gentle boi -- do not let the soup boil for more than a minute or it will lose its clear red color.
4. Grate the beets from one or two cans into the soup.
5. Add lemon juice and seasonings to taste. Reheat before serving, making sure not to bring to a boil.
6. Place 5 or 6 uszka dumplings in each bowl before serving and pour barszcz over them (uszka recipe follows).

Uszka - Polish Mushroom Dumplings

Stuffing Ingredients:

16 oz. fresh mushrooms, finely chopped
1 stick butter
1 medium-sized onion, finely chopped
white of one hard-boiled egg, finely chopped
2 tbsps. breadcrumbs
1 tbsp. parsley, chopped
Salt and pepper to taste

Directions:

1. Sauté the mushrooms and onions in the butter for 10-15 minutes.
2. Add bread crumbs, finely chopped egg white, and parsley.
3. Mix well and add salt and pepper to taste.

Dough Ingredients:

1 egg yolk
2 cups of white flour, sifted
1/2 cup lukewarm water

Directions:

1. Mix the flour with the egg yolk, adding water slowly and working it into the dough until a soft mass is formed.
2. Keep kneading until the dough no longer sticks to your fingers.
3. Roll dough into a ball and cover with flour.
4. Place in a bowl covered with plastic and refrigerate for an hour.
5. Roll out a third of the dough into a thin layer on a floured surface and cut into 1 1/2 inch squares.

6. Place a spoonful of the mushroom filling in the center of the square of dough, fold in half to form a triangle, and press the edges tightly to close. Then bring two corners of the triangle together and press tightly.
7. Place dumplings on a floured dishcloth and cover with another cloth until ready to cook.
8. Repeat with rest of dough.
9. Cook dumplings in batches in boiling, salted water for 5 minutes, until they float to the top.
10. Take out with slotted spoon and toss in meted butter.
11. Serve immediately with barszcz or refrigerate and reheat gently before serving.

Fish in Aspic - Ryba w Galarecie

Ingredients:

1 large carp, cleaned
1 tbsp. gelatin
4 cups vegetable stock
2 tbsps. water
4 peppercorns
1 egg white
3 bay leaves

Directions:

1. Remove head from fish.
2. Cook head and spices in vegetable stock for half an hour. Strain the stock and set aside.
3. Place whole fish in a shallow roaster of fish pan.
4. Cover with strained stock and simmer for half hour until tender.
5. Remove fish and place on a serving platter.
6. To clarify stock, add slightly beaten egg white to the stock and bring to boiling point, stirring lightly. Strain through cheesecloth.
7. Dissolve gelatin in two tbsps. water in a large bowl; add stock.
8. Pour over the cooled fish. Chill thoroughly until firm. Garnish with carrot rings, hardboiled eggs, and lemon slices.

Polish Rolled Herring - Rolmops

Ingredients:
4 pickled herring filets, each cut into 3 thin pieces
Pickling juices from jar reserved
Dill pickles quartered and cut into one-inch pieces
Pickled onions
Dill or parsley for garnish

Directions:
1. Place a piece of pickle and a pickled onion at one end of a herring piece.
2. Roll the herring tightly and skewer with a toothpick to hold the roll together.
3. Before serving, drizzle rolls with some of the pickling juice from the herring jar, insert a few small sprigs of fresh dill or parsley into an open end of each roll and serve with rye bread or pumpernickel as an appetizer before Wigilia.

Polish Pike - Szczupak po Polsku

Ingredients:

2 carrots
2 celery stalks
1 onion, quartered
10 peppercorns
1 bay leaf
2 tsps. salt
1 large whole fish (pike, whitefish, or sole)

Topping Ingredients:

1/4 cup butter
4 tbsps. fresh dill, chopped
1 tsp. salt
1/2 tsp. pepper
1/4 cup lemon juice
6 hardboiled eggs, finely chopped

Directions:

1. Place vegetables, fish, dry seasonings, and enough water to cover the fish in a saucepan or shallow fish pan.
2. Boil gently for about 15 to 20 minutes or until the fish flakes easily.
3. For the topping, heat the butter in a skillet and add the chopped eggs, lemon juice, dill, salt, and pepper.
4. Cook 5 minutes, stirring frequently.
5. When the fish is cooked, remove it gently from the fish pan and set on a warm platter.
6. Spoon the topping over the fish and serve immediately.

Sauerkraut with Mushrooms - Kapusta z Grzybami

Ingredients:

2 oz. dried mushrooms
16 oz. fresh mushrooms (portabella mushrooms preferred)
1 large onion
4 tbsps. butter
1 1/2 pounds sauerkraut, rinsed in cold water, and drained
1/3 cup water
2 tbsps. flour
salt and pepper

Directions:

1. Soak the dried mushrooms in 2 cups of hot water for 2 hours drain, and squeeze dry in a cheesecloth.
2. Chop finely.
3. Wash and coarsely chop the fresh mushrooms and onion and sauté in the butter in a skillet for 5-7 minutes.
4. Add sauerkraut to mushrooms; cook and stir for another 10 minutes.
5. Blend 1/3 cup water into flour, beating gently to remove lumps.
6. Add slowly to sauerkraut and simmer for 15 minutes.
7. Season to taste with salt and pepper.

Noodles with Cabbage - Kluski z kapusta

Ingredients:

1 lb. kluski-style noodles (or rotini), cooked and drained
2 sticks butter
1 large onion, coarsely chopped
2 lbs. sauerkraut, drained (rinsed or unrinsed as desired)
1 lb. fresh mushrooms
Salt and pepper to taste

Directions:

1. In a large frying pan, sautéthe onion in one stick of butter until golden but not browned.
2. Add sauerkraut and cook over medium heat for 10-15 minutes until warmed, stirring frequently.
3. Place in a large bowl. Clean and trim mushrooms and cut into thick slices.
4. Sauté mushrooms in remaining butter in a large frying pan for 5-7 minutes and add to bowl with sauerkraut.
5. Mix gently, check for seasoning, and then place into a buttered casserole and bake for 40-45 minutes in a preheated oven at 350 degrees.

Mushroom Cabbage Rolls - Golabki z Grzybami

Ingredients:

1 large cabbage (with big leaves)
1 cup uncooked long grain rice
2 large onions, finely chopped
16 oz. fresh mushrooms
2 oz. dried mushrooms (optional)
1 stick of butter
6 cups of tomato juice or mushroom stock
salt and pepper to taste

Directions:

1. Take out the hard core of the cabbage with a sharp knife.
2. Place the cabbage in a large pot of salted, lightly boiling water for approximately 10 minutes.
3. When the outside leaves are tender, peel them off gently with a fork.
4. Cook the rice according to package instructions until just tender and set aside.
5. If using dried mushrooms, soak them in hot water for two hours.
6. Drain, squeeze out excess water, and chop finely.
7. Wash and chop the fresh mushrooms. Sauté the onions in half of the butter until softened and then add mushrooms.
8. Cook for another 10 minutes, adding more butter as needed.
9. Add mushrooms and onions to the cooked rice, mix and season well.
10. Place two tbsps. of the mushroom and rice mixture in each cabbage leaf and wrap it carefully, rolling the leaf and folding the ends under tightly, like a parcel.
11. Heat the oven to 350 degrees.
12. Grease a deep roasting pan or large casserole and fill it with the cabbage rolls, packing them tightly together.

13. Pour enough tomato juice or mushroom stock to cover the rolls.
14. Cover tightly with foil and bake in oven for 40 minutes. Uncover and bake for another 10-15 minutes to brown the rolls lightly.
15. Serve with sour cream or mushroom sauce.

Polish Dumplings - Pierogi

Ingredients:

Pierogi Dough Ingredients:

2 cups all purpose flour
2 eggs
2 tbsps. sour cream
1/2 tsp. salt
1/2 cup lukewarm water

Directions:

1. Mound flour on a large cutting board and make a well in the center.
2. Drop eggs, sour cream, and salt into well.
3. Add water a few drops at a time and work it into the flour with a knife, moving slowly from the center to the outside of the flour mound.
4. While mixing the liquid into the flour with one hand, keep the flour mounded with other hand.
5. Try not to let any liquid break through the walls of the mound.
6. When all the water and egg is mixed into the flour, knead until the dough is firm and well mixed and no longer sticks to yours hands (about 10-15 minutes).
7. Add flour if it seems too sticky; a few drops of water if it seems too dry. Then cover the dough with a bowl or clean dishtowel and let rest for 30 minutes.
8. Divide the dough into halves. On a well-floured surface, using half of the dough at a time, roll it out as thinly as possible.
9. Cut out 3-inch rounds with a biscuit cutter or a drinking glass. Then place a tbsp. of filling in the middle of each round of dough, fold over carefully and press edges together. Be sure to press firmly as filling will spill out during cooking if the dough rounds are not well sealed.
10. Pierogi can be frozen at this point.

11. Layer carefully in freezer container, be sure to separate layers with wax paper. If you are going to eat right away, drop 12-20 pierogi into a large pot of boiling, lightly salted water.
12. Cook gently 3 to 5 minutes, or until pierogi float.
13. Lift out of water with perforated spoon.
14. Toss in butter and place in heatproof serving dish.
15. Pierogi can be reheated in the microwave or in the oven, just before serving. They can also be reheated by frying in butter.
16. Serve pierogi with sour cream and chopped chives.

Sauerkraut and Mushroom Filling

Ingredients:

2 cups sauerkraut
2 tbsps. butter
1/2 cup chopped onion
4 oz. mushrooms
1/4 tsp. pepper
1 hardboiled egg, finely chopped
1 tbsp. breadcrumbs
2 tbsps. sour cream

Directions:

1. Rinse sauerkraut in cold water and drain well. Sauté for 10 minutes in medium saucepan until dry.
2. Set aside. In frying pan, sauté onion and mushrooms in the remaining butter.
3. Add sauerkraut and pepper.
4. Fry until sauerkraut is golden.
5. Add chopped egg, breadcrumbs, and sour cream.
6. Mix. Cool thoroughly before stuffing pierogi.

Potato and Cheese Filling

Ingredients:

4 Russet potatoes
8 oz. farmer's cheese or dry cottage cheese
1 onion, finely chopped
2 tbsps. butter
Salt and pepper to taste

Directions:

1. Peel and boil the potatoes until tender.
2. Mash until smooth and let cool. Sauté chopped onion in the butter.
3. Let cool. When mashed potatoes are cool, add onions and cheese.
4. Mix well.
5. Add salt and pepper to taste before filling pierogi.
6. Serve with sour cream.

Cheese Filling Ingredients:

8 oz. dry cottage cheese, farmer's cheese, or ricotta.
1 egg
2 tbsps. sugar (to taste)
1/2 tsp. vanilla extract
1/2 cup raisins (optional)

Directions:

1. Mix well before stuffing pierogi.
2. If using raisins, soak them in warm water for one hour and drain and dry well before adding to cheese mixture.

Noodles with Poppy Seeds - Kluski z Makiem

Ingredients:

1 cup boiling water
4 tbsps. poppy seeds
3 tbsps. sugar
1 package wide egg noodles, kluski
2-3 tbsps. melted butter

Directions:

1. Scald poppy seeds with boiling water and soak for 3 hours.
2. Drain. Force through food grinder (or coffee grinder) and mix with sugar.
3. Cook noodles in lightly salted water.
4. Drain and rinse with cold water.
5. Toss noodles in melted butter, place in shallow baking dish, and keep in warm oven until ready to serve.
6. Toss with poppy seeds and sugar just before serving.

Dried Fruit Compote - Kompot z Owocow Suszonych

Ingredients:

1 1/2 pounds mixed dried fruit
6 cups of water
1 lemon
6 whole cloves, 1 cinnamon stick
1 cup of sugar

Directions:

1. Rinse and soak fruit in 4 cups of water overnight in a ceramic or glass bowl.
2. Transfer fruit and the water into to a stainless steel or enameled pot, add 2 more cups water, sugar, cloves, and cinnamon.
3. Peel the lemon, leaving the peel in one piece, if possible, and add the peel to the pot.
4. Then cut the peeled lemon in half and squeeze the juice into the pot.
5. Cook for 30 minutes, adding more water, lemon juice, or water to taste.
6. Refrigerate for a few hours.
7. Serve cold in glass bowls, along with Christmas cookies, for dessert.

Christmas Wheat Berry Pudding - Kutia

Ingredients:

1 cup whole wheat berries
2 cups hot water
1/2 cup poppy seeds
1/2 cup slivered almonds
1/2 cup white raisins
1 shot vodka, rum, or brandy (optional)
1/2 cup honey
Extra honey and heavy cream, for serving

Directions:

1. Soak wheat berries in two cups of hot water for two hours or overnight.
2. Drain wheat berries and place in an enameled pot.
3. Cover with cold water, bring to a boil, reduce heat, and cook over low heat for two hours, or until all liquid is absorbed. Let cool.
4. Cover poppy seeds with a cup of boiling water for 30 minutes.
5. Drain through a fine sieve and place in a glass bowl to dry.
6. Grind poppy seeds in a coffee grinder or food processor, until the seeds start to show their white interiors.
7. Add ground poppy seeds to the wheat berries and then add almonds, raisins, and honey.
8. Mix well.
9. Add more honey if needed. Refrigerate.
10. Serve kutia cold in small glass bowls with extra honey on the side.
11. Add 2-3 tbsps. of heavy cream (or half and half) to each serving.

Polish Almond Soup - Zupa migdalowa

This soup is often served during Wigilia, between courses or after the family comes home from Midnight Mass typically served at the beginning of the meal.

Ingredients:

5 cups whole milk
1/2 pound finely ground almonds
1 tsp. almond extract
2 cups cooked rice
1/3 cup sugar

Directions:

1. In a large saucepan, bring the milk to a very low boil.
2. Add the remaining ingredients and continue cooking, over low heat, for 5-7 minutes, stirring constantly until the rice is warm.
3. Add more sugar to taste. You can garnish with raisins, cinnamon, or sliced almonds before serving.

Polish Honey Spice Cookies - Pierniczki

These cookies are very popular in Poland during the holidays. They are very similar to American gingerbread cookies. To hang decorated pierniczki on your Christmas tree, the way it is done in Poland, you should make a hole in the cookies before baking with a plastic straw. After baking, decorate and thread a thin ribbon through the hole in the cookie to hang it on your tree.

Ingredients:

1 cup honey
4 cups flour
4 eggs
1 cup sugar
pinch of ground black pepper
1/2 tbsp. ground cinnamon
1/2 tbsp. ground nutmeg
1/2 tbsp. ground cloves
1/2 tbsp. ground allspice
1 tbsp. baking soda

Directions:

1. Heat the honey in a small saucepan until it just begins to boil.
2. Take off heat and allow to cool slightly.
3. Combine eggs and sugar in a bowl and beat together until slightly thickened.
4. In another bowl, mix the flour, spices, and baking soda together and add slowly to the egg and sugar mixture while beating rapidly. The dough should not have any lumps.
5. Pour in the lukewarm honey and mix everything until smooth.
6. You can cover the dough with plastic and refrigerate until ready to make the cookies.

7. Turn out the dough onto a lightly floured surface, knead for a minute to warm it, and then roll out with a floured rolling pin to a thickness of a 1/4 inch. Use cookie cutters to cut into shapes.
8. Bake in 350 degree preheated oven on greased cookie sheets for about 12 minutes.
9. Allow to cool completely before decorating.

Polish Kolaczki Cookies - Kolaczki

Ingredients:

1 (8-oz.) cream cheese, softened
12 oz. (3 sticks) unsalted butter, softened
3 cups all-purpose flour
2 (14-oz.) cans fillings of choice (apricot, prune, raspberry, etc.)
Confectioners' sugar

Directions:

1. Mix cream cheese and butter until light and fluffy.
2. Add flour 1 cup at a time and mix well.
3. Wrap dough in plastic and refrigerate for at least 1 hour.
4. Heat oven to 350 degrees.
5. Roll out dough 1/4-inch on a surface that has been dusted with equal parts confectioners' and granulated sugar (not flour).
6. Cut into 2-inch squares.
7. Place 1/2 to 1 tsp. filling on center of each square. Overlap opposite corners of dough to the center over filling.
8. Bake for 15 minutes or until corners start to brown.
9. Cool and dust with confectioners' sugar.
10. Dust with confectioners' sugar just before serving.

Polish Dried Mushroom Soup - Zupa Grzybowa

Ingredients:

4 oz. dried mushrooms (Polish borowiki or dried Italian porcini mushrooms)
3 1/2 cups water (hot)
3 quarts beef stock
1 cup pearl barley (optional)
2 cups sour cream
2 tbsps. all-purpose flour
Salt and pepper to taste
Sour cream, for garnish
Chopped parsley, for garnish
Kluski noodles, optional

Directions:

1. Combine mushrooms and hot water in a large, heatproof bowl. Let stand 1 hour. With your fingers, work mushrooms to release any grit. Let stand until very pliable, about 1 hour longer.
2. Lift mushrooms from the liquid.
3. Cut mushrooms into large pieces and set aside. Reserve bowl of soaking liquid.
4. In a 5- to 6-quart pot, combine stock and chopped mushrooms.
5. Pour reserved soaking liquid into the pot, taking care not to disturb grit in the bowl.
6. Rinse and drain barley and add to the pot, if using.
7. Cover and bring to a boil.
8. Reduce heat and simmer, covered until barley is tender to the bite, about 1 hour.
9. In a medium bowl, mix sour cream with flour and temper by whisking in a little hot soup.
10. Pour contents of the bowl into hot soup, whisking constantly on medium-high heat until it comes to a boil. Adjust seasonings.

11. Remove from heat and ladle into warm bowls.
12. Serve with kluski noodles, if desired. Garnish with sour cream and parsley, if desired.

Polish Pickle Soup - Zupa Ogórkowa

Ingredients:

8 cups chicken or vegetable stock
1 pound potatoes (peeled and quartered)
2 large carrots (peeled and diced)
1 large parsnip peeled and diced
1 rib celery (diced)
6 dill pickles (shredded)
1 cup sour cream
Optional garnish: fresh dill, chopped

Directions:

1. In a large saucepan, bring the stock to a boil.
2. Add potatoes, carrots, parsnip and celery. Return to the boil, reduce heat and simmer until vegetables are tender.
3. Add pickles and any accumulated juices and combine well.
4. Temper the sour cream in a small heatproof bowl by adding a few ladles of hot soup and whisking constantly.
5. Transfer the tempered sour cream back to the soup and heat through until starting to simmer but do not boil or the sour cream will break.
6. Serve hot in heated bowls with chopped fresh dill and slices of rye bread with caraway seeds.

Polish Potato Soup - Zupa Ziemniaczana

Ingredients:

4 oz. bacon (about 4 strips, diced)
2 large onions (finely chopped)
2 large carrots (peeled and finely chopped)
1 rib celery (finely chopped)
2 pounds potatoes (peeled, cut into 1 1/2-inch cubes)
8 cups chicken stock (or vegetable stock, hot)
4 tbsps. fresh parsley (chopped)
1 bay leaf
Salt and black pepper to taste

Directions:

1. In a large saucepan, cook bacon until it begins to render some of its fat.
2. Add onions and sauté until translucent.
3. Add carrots, celery, and potatoes and sauté gently for 5 minutes, but do not brown.
4. Then add hot stock, parsley and bay leaf.
5. Bring to a boil.
6. Reduce heat and simmer, covered, for about 20 minutes or until vegetables are tender.
7. Remove bay leaf, adjust seasonings, and serve hot with additional chopped parsley (if desired) and light rye bread.
8. Note: If desired, the soup can be creamed by fork blending 2 tbsps. all-purpose flour with 1 cup sour cream and tempering it with a few ladles of hot soup.
9. Return tempered sour cream to soup pot and stir in until the soup simmers but does not boil.

Polish Tomato-Rice Soup - Zupa Pomidorowa Ryzu

Ingredients:

2 tbsps. butter
1 large chopped onion
2 sliced ribs celery
2 large peeled and sliced carrots
1 clove minced garlic
6 cups chicken or vegetable stock
2 pounds peeled, seeded and chopped tomatoes
1/2 tsp. crushed thyme leaves
Salt and pepper to taste
1 cup cooked and cooled rice
1/2 cup sweet or sour cream (optional)

Directions:

1. In a large saucepan or Dutch oven, sauté onion, celery, carrots and garlic until onion is translucent.
2. Add stock, tomatoes, thyme, and salt and pepper to taste.
3. Bring to a boil, reduce heat, and simmer uncovered 1 hour or until carrots are tender and soup has reduced somewhat.
4. At this point, the soup can be pureed, if desired.
5. Add rice and heat through. If desired, sweet or sour cream can be added at this point.

Polish Barley Soup - Krupnik

Ingredients:

1 oz. Polish borowiki mushrooms (dried)
3 tbsps. olive oil
2 large yellow onions (chopped)
3 garlic cloves (minced)
3 tbsps. fresh parsley (chopped)
10 cups whey (or chicken, beef or vegetable broth or water)
1 cup rinsed pearl barley
4 peeled medium carrots (sliced into 1/2-inch rounds)
4 peeled medium potatoes (diced)
1 bay leaf
2 tbsps. Vegeta seasoning
Pepper (to taste)

Directions:

1. Place dried mushrooms in a heatproof bowl and pour 2 cups boiling water over. Let soak while you continue with the rest of the recipe.
2. In a large saucepan or Dutch oven, heat olive oil until it shimmers.
3. Add onion and garlic and sauté until translucent, about 7 minutes.
4. Add parsley, whey or broth, drained barley, carrots, potatoes, bay leaf, Vegeta and pepper.
5. Lift mushrooms from soaking liquid being careful not to pick up the grit with the mushrooms.
6. Slice mushrooms and add to pot.
7. Bring to a boil, reduce heat and simmer for 1 hour or until barley is tender.
8. If desired, the carefully strained mushroom-soaking liquid can be added to the soup. Otherwise save it to make a delicious mushroom sauce, adding fresh, sautéed mushrooms.
9. Serve the soup with a dollop of sour cream if you like and a hearty bread of choice.

Polish Split Pea Soup - Zupa Grochowka

Ingredients:

3 slices bacon, cut in half
1 finely chopped garlic clove
1 large onion, chopped
3 celery stalks, trimmed and cut into 1/2-inch pieces
3 large carrots, peeled and cut into 1/2-inch pieces
8 cups water
1 (1-pound) bag green or yellow split peas, rinsed
1 meaty ham bone
1 bay leaf
1 cup chopped ham
2 large potatoes, peeled and cut into 1-inch pieces
Salt and pepper to taste

Directions:

1. In a large stock pot, fry bacon until fully cooked.
2. Remove, crumble when cool and set aside.
3. Add garic, onion, celery and carrots to bacon grease in pot and sauté over medium heat until limp.
4. Add water, peas, ham bone and bay leaf.
5. Bring to a boil, skimming any foam that rises to the top.
6. Add the chopped ham, potatoes, crumbled bacon, salt and pepper to taste, and return to a boil.
7. Reduce to a simmer, cover and cook on low for 1 hour or until peas have completely broken down, stirring frequently to avoid scorching.

Polish Beets with Sour Cream - Buraczki ze Smietana

Ingredients:
4 medium beets
For the Dressing:
1 cup sour cream
1 tsp. sugar
Salt and black pepper to taste
Garnish: fresh dill sprigs or chopped dill

Directions:
1. Mash the beets and pat them dry.
2. Boil or roast them in their jackets until a thin knife tip can be inserted easily into the flesh, but they are still somewhat al dente.
3. When they are cool enough to handle, peel them and set aside until they finish cooling.
4. Cut cooled beets into strips or julienne.

Dressing Directions:
1. In a medium bowl, combine sour cream, sugar, and salt and pepper to taste, mixing well.
2. Fold julienned beets into the dressing being careful not to break up the beets.
3. If serving hot, transfer mixture to a saucepan and warm just until you notice small bubbles starting to appear around the edges.
4. You don't want to bring to a boil because the sour cream will break.
5. If serving cold, cover the bowl you mixed the beets in and refrigerate until thoroughly cold.
6. Transfer the beet mixture to a serving bowl and garnish with dill sprigs or chopped fresh dill.

Note: You can speed things up by using 2 cups well-drained canned or jarred sliced beets and cutting them into julienne strips.

Polish Cucumbers in Sour Cream

Cucumber Ingredients:

1 large cucumber, trimmed and peeled
Salt

Dressing Ingredients:

1/2 cup sour cream
1 tsp. sugar
2 tsps. white vinegar, optional
1 tbsp. fresh dill, chopped

Directions:

1. Marinate the cucumbers.
2. Run a channel knife or fork down the length of the cucumbers to produce a pretty edge, and slice thinly.
3. Place in a colander over a bowl to catch the juices and salt the cucumbers liberally. Allow to stand for 30 minutes.
4. Make the Dressing
5. While the cucumbers are marinating, make the dressing.
6. In a small bowl, mix together sour cream, sugar, optional vinegar, and dill until well blended.
7. Refrigerate covered until ready to assemble the salad.
8. Assemble the Salad
9. Pat cucumbers dry and place in a medium bowl.
10. Add the dressing and toss with the cucumber slices.
11. Season to taste with salt and black pepper.
12. Chill until very cold and sprinkle with additional dill, if desired, before serving.

Polish Creamed Beet Barszcz Soup - Barszcz Zabielany

Ingredients:

4 beets, washed, or 2 cups sliced canned or jarred beets
4 cups stock (meat or vegetable)
1 tsp. sugar
Dash salt and black pepper
1/2 cup sour cream
2 tbsps. all-purpose flour

Directions:

1. Heat oven to 400 F.
2. Wrap beets in aluminum foil and roast until tender, about 30 to 45 minutes. When cool enough to handle, peel and slice.
3. In a medium pot, bring the stock to a boil, add the beets, sugar, and salt and pepper to taste.
4. Bring to a boil, reduce heat and simmer 10 minutes.
5. Transfer to a blender or food processor and puré until smooth, and return to pot.
6. Mix sour cream with flour until well blended. Temper the sour cream mixture with a ladle of hot soup, whisking constantly. Transfer the tempered sour cream to remaining soup and whisk until smooth.
7. Simmer to cook out the raw flour taste and until the soup is thickened, but do not boil vigorously.
8. Serve immediately or cool quickly in an ice-water bath and refrigerate to serve cold.
9. Garnish with dill, julienned beets, and sour cream.

Polish Light Rye Bread with Caraway Seeds

Ingredients:

2 cups milk (scalded)
2 tbsps. butter
2 tbsps. sugar
1 tsp. salt
1 package active dry yeast
1/2 cup water (lukewarm)
4 cups rye flour
2 1/2 cups whole-wheat flour
2 tbsps. caraway seeds, optional
1 egg white, beaten for egg wash

Directions:

1. In a heatproof large bowl or the bowl of a stand mixer, pour scalded milk over butter, sugar, and salt.
2. Stir and cool.
3. Dissolve yeast in lukewarm water.
4. Add softened yeast and 3 cups rye flour to the milk mixture. Using the paddle attachment of your stand mixer, or by hand, beat thoroughly.
5. Add the remaining rye flour and beat again until flour is thoroughly combined.
6. Scrape dough out into a clean, greased bowl, cover and let rise in warm place until doubled in bulk, about 1 hour, or follow this quick tip to cut the rise time.
7. Scrape dough back into clean stand mixer bowl and, using the dough hook, knead in the whole-wheat flour and caraway seed, if using, until dough is smooth.
8. Alternatively, the kneading can be done by hand on a well-floured surface.
9. Divide the dough in half and shape into 2 oblong or round loaves.

10. Place loaves on parchment-lined or greased baking sheets. Bread can also be placed in greased 9-inch-by-5-inch loaf pans or 9-inch round pans.
11. Cover and let rise in warm place until doubled in bulk, about 1 hour.
12. Meanwhile, heat oven to 450 degrees. Brush the loaves with beaten egg white and bake for 15 minutes.
13. Reduce heat to 350 degrees and bake 35 to 40 minutes longer or until an instant-read thermometer inserted in the center of the loaves registers 190 degrees.
14. Remove from the oven and cool on wire racks.
15. Store in an airtight container or slice loaves and freeze.

Note: If a more tender crust is desired, brush loaves with melted butter 5 minutes before removing from the oven.

Split Peas and Cabbage - Kapusta z Grochem

Ingredients:

1 pound dried yellow split peas (rinsed and drained)
3 cups boiling water
1 small head cabbage (shredded)
1-quart sauerkraut (undrained or drained, if desired, reserving some of the kraut juice)
3 cups water
1 onion, chopped fine
2 tbsps. butter
Salt and black pepper to taste
1/2 pound bacon, chopped

Directions:

1. Combine peas and boiling water in a small saucepan.
2. Bring to a boil over medium-high heat and continue boiling 2 minutes.
3. Remove from heat.
4. Cover and let soak 30 minutes.
5. Bring to a boil again.
6. Reduce heat to a simmer, cover and cook 20 minutes, or until cooked down into a purée, adding more water if necessary.
7. Remove from heat and set aside.
8. Meanwhile, in a large pot or Dutch oven, place shredded cabbage, sauerkraut, and 3 cups water.
9. Bring to a boil.
10. Reduce heat to a simmer, cover and cook 1 hour.
11. While cabbage is cooking, sauté onion in butter until golden brown but not burned.
12. Set aside.
13. Add cooked peas to cabbage mixture.
14. Season to taste with salt and pepper.
15. Add some kraut juice or vegetable broth if too dry.
16. Add sautéed onions and mix well.

17. Heat until warm throughout and serve.
18. Add to cabbage with cooked peas.

Polish Sweet-Sour Red Cabbage - Czerwona Kapusta Zasmażana

Ingredients:

1 (3-pound) head red cabbage, washed, dried, cored and shredded
1 medium onion, shredded
2 tbsps. butter or canola oil
1 cup water
4 tbsps. red-wine vinegar
4 tbsps. brown sugar
1/2 tsp. black pepper
1 tsp. salt

Directions:

1. In a large pot or Dutch oven, cook cabbage and onion in butter or oil on medium heat until it collapses, about 5 minutes.
2. Meanwhile, in a small bowl, mix together water, vinegar, brown sugar, pepper, and salt until sugar is dissolved.
3. Add to cabbage mixture.
4. Bring to a boil.
5. Reduce heat to medium-low.
6. Continue to cook, stirring occasionally, until cabbage is tender, about 15 minutes.
7. Refrigerate overnight to improve flavor. Freezes well.

Sausage and Noodle Casserole

Ingredients:

8 oz. egg noodles
1 pound ground sausage
1/2 cup chopped onion
1/4 cup chopped green bell pepper
1 (10 3/4 oz) can cream of chicken soup
1/2 cup water
1/4 tsp. salt (or to taste)
freshly ground black pepper, to taste
1/2-1 cup French fried onions, crumbled

Directions:

1. Heat the oven to 350 degrees F.
2. Lightly butter a shallow 2-quart baking dish or spray it with cooking oil spray.
3. Cook the noodles in a saucepan of boiling salted water following the package directions.
4. Drain in a colander and set aside.
5. Crumble the sausage into a large skillet and add the chopped onion and green bell pepper.
6. Place the skillet over medium heat and cook, stirring, until the sausage has browned and vegetables are tender.
7. Drain off excess drippings.
8. In a large bowl, combine the sausage mixture with the cream of chicken soup, water, and cooked noodles.
9. Taste and add salt and pepper, as needed.
10. Spoon the mixture into the prepared baking dish.
11. Sprinkle with crumbled onion rings.
12. Bake in the preheated oven for about 30 minutes, or until hot and bubbly.

Polish Cabbage Potato Casserole

Ingredients:

1 pound diced bacon
1 large diced onion
1 (2 1/2-pound) cabbage, cored and coarsely chopped
3 large russet potatoes, peeled, cut into 1/2-inch cubes and parboiled
1 tsp. salt (or to taste)
1/2 to 1 tsp. pepper (or to taste)
1/2 cup heavy cream
1/2 cup shredded Polish Koldamer or Kurpianka cheese or Swiss cheese

Directions:

1. Heat oven to 375 degrees.
2. In a very large ovenproof skillet or Dutch oven, sauté diced bacon until crisp but not burned. Using a slotted spoon, remove bacon, and set aside.
3. If desired, some of the bacon fat can be removed but, traditionally, it is left in.
4. Add the onion and cabbage to the bacon fat, mixing well.
5. Cook until the cabbage has completely collapsed and is al dente, about 20 minutes.
6. Add the well-drained potatoes, salt, pepper, cream, and reserved bacon, and mix completely.
7. Remove from heat.
8. Sprinkle the cheese over the cabbage-potato-bacon casserole and cover tightly with foil or an ovenproof lid.
9. Bake 35 minutes or until potatoes are almost done.
10. Remove cover and bake an additional 10 minutes or until cheese is melted and golden, and potatoes are tender.

Polish Haluski - Noodles, Onion and Cabbage

Ingredients:

1 very large onion, sliced into rounds
8 oz. butter
1 large head cabbage, cut into 1-inch pieces
Salt and pepper
2 tbsps. water, as needed
8 oz. 1/2-inch egg noodles, cooked

Directions:

1. Cut the round onion slices in half and then in half again so each round yields four pieces.
2. In a large skillet or Dutch oven, sauté onion in 4 oz. of butter, stirring frequently, over low heat until very lightly caramelized. This could take 15 minutes or more.
3. Add the 1-inch cabbage pieces and remaining 4 oz. butter, salt and pepper to taste, and 2 tbsps. of water, if necessary.
4. Do not cover.
5. Sauté slowly, stirring frequently, over low heat until cabbage is tender but not brown (cook to al dente stage if baking in the oven).
6. This could take 30 minutes or more.
7. Combine onion-cabbage mixture with 8 oz. cooked noodles, mixing well.
8. Adjust seasonings and serve. or, heat oven to 350 degrees.
9. Butter a large gratin pan and turn the mixture into it.
10. Bake uncovered 30 minutes or until top is lightly browned.
11. Serve immediately.
12. Note: If this dish is intended to be a meal with meat, the onions can be sautéed in diced bacon instead of the butter.

Polish Sausage Casserole

Ingredients:
1 tbsp. butter
2 large onions, chopped
1 medium head cabbage, chopped or shredded
2 apples (red-skinned, cored and sliced 1/2-inch thick, peels can be left on, if desired)
2 large potatoes (russet, peels can be left on if desired, parboiled for 5 minutes, save the cooking water, and coarsely chopped)
1 tbsp. seasoning (Vegeta or Maggi)
Pinch black pepper
1 tbsp. caraway seeds, or to taste
1 pound smoked Polish sausage (skin removed, if desired, cut into 6 pieces and scored diagonally 3 times)

Directions:
1. In a large, dutch oven or skillet with a lid, sauté onion in butter over medium heat until translucent.
2. Then, without stirring, add cabbage and sprinkle evenly with Vegeta or Maggi seasoning.
3. Add apples, caraway, and pepper without stirring.
4. Top with sausage and 1 cup of the cooking water from potatoes.
5. Cover. When the water begins to boil, reduce heat and simmer 10 minutes.
6. Uncover and mix all ingredients together.
7. Replace cover and simmer 10 minutes more.
8. Remove the cover and test for doneness of the cabbage.
9. If there are too many juices, cook over low heat until reduced.

Polish Nalesniki

Ingredients:

2 cups ricotta cheese
3 oz. cream cheese, softened
1 egg yolk
2 tbsps. butter, melted
1 tbsp. white sugar
1 tsp. vanilla extract
1/2 tsp. salt
12 crepes
1 tbsp. butter, divided

Directions:

1. Process ricotta cheese and cream cheese in a food processor until smooth and creamy; add egg yolk, melted butter, sugar, vanilla extract, and salt and process until fluffy.
2. Divide cheese mixture between the crepes.
3. Spread filling into a thin layer and roll crepes around the filling.
4. Melt 1 tsp. butter in a skillet over medium heat.
5. Fry 3 crepes in melted butter until heated through, 1 to 2 minutes per side; repeat with remaining butter and crepes.

Polish Sweet Bread

Ingredients:

1 1/2 cups milk
4 tbsps. butter
2 eggs, beaten
1/2 cup white sugar
1 tsp. vanilla extract
4 cups bread flour
3 tsps. active dry yeast
1 tsp. salt
1/4 cup white sugar
1/4 cup brown sugar
1/3 cup bread flour
1/4 cup butter 1 egg
1 tbsp. water

Directions:

1. Warm the milk in a small saucepan until it bubbles, then remove from heat.
2. Mix in the 4 tbsps. butter; stir until melted. Let cool until lukewarm.
3. Pour milk mixture into bread machine pan.
4. Add 2 eggs, 1/2 cup sugar, vanilla extract, 4 cups bread flour, yeast and salt.
5. Choose Dough setting; press start.
6. When dough is finished mixing, leave it in the bread machine pan and cover with a towel. Let rise until doubled, about 45 minutes.
7. Deflate the dough and turn it out onto a lightly floured surface.
8. Divide the dough into two equal pieces and form into loaves.
9. Place the loaves into two lightly greased 9x5 inch loaf pans.
10. Cover the loaves with a damp cloth and let rise until doubled in volume, about 40 minutes.
11. Meanwhile, preheat oven to 350 degrees F (175 degrees C).

12. In a small bowl, combine 1/4 cup sugar, 1/4 brown sugar and 1/3 cup flour.
13. Cut in butter until mixture resembles coarse crumbs; set aside.
14. In a separate bowl, beat together 1 egg and 1 tbsp. water.
15. Brush loaves of risen bread with the egg wash and then sprinkle on crumb topping.
16. Bake at 350 degrees for about 30 minutes, until golden brown.

Polish Sourdough Rye Bread

Ingredients:

2 (.25 oz.) packages active dry yeast
1 tsp. white sugar
2 cups water
4 cups rye flour
1 cup buttermilk, room temperature
1 tsp. baking soda
1 tbsp. salt
8 cups bread flour
1 tbsp. caraway seed

Directions:

1. The night before making the bread, in a medium sized mixing bowl, dissolve one packet of yeast and the sugar in 2 cups of water.
2. Let stand until creamy, about 10 minutes.
3. Stir in the rye flour until the mixture is smooth.
4. Cover and let stand overnight.
5. The next day, dissolve the remaining package of yeast in the buttermilk.
6. Add the rye flour mixture, the baking soda, the salt, 4 cups of the bread flour and stir to combine.
7. Add the remaining 4 cups of bread flour, 1/2 cup at a time, stirring well after each addition (you may not need to add all of the flour).
8. When the dough has become a smooth and coherent mass, turn it out onto a lightly floured surface and knead until smooth and supple, about 8 minutes.
9. Sprinkle the caraway seeds on the dough and knead them in until they are evenly distributed throughout the dough.
10. Lightly oil a large mixing bowl.
11. Place the dough in the bowl and turn to coat with the oil.
12. Cover with a damp cloth and let rise in a warm place for about 1 hour or until the volume has doubled.
13. Preheat oven to 350 degrees F (175 degrees C).

14. Turn the dough onto a lightly floured surface and divide into three pieces.
15. Form each piece into a loaf and place in 3 lightly greased 9x5 inch bread pans.
16. Cover and let rise until nearly doubled, about 1 hour.
17. Bake at 350 degrees F (175 degrees C) for about 35 minutes or until the bottom of the loaves sound hollow when tapped.

Polish Cream Cheese Coffee Cake

Ingredients:

1 cup white sugar
1/2 cup butter
1 egg
1 cup sour cream
1 tsp. vanilla extract
3 cups all-purpose flour
1 tsp. baking soda
1 tsp. baking powder

Filling Ingredients:

2 (8 oz.) packages cream cheese, softened
1/2 cup white sugar
1 egg

Topping Ingredients :

1/2 cup chopped pecans
1/2 cup brown sugar
1/3 cup all-purpose flour
1/3 cup butter

Directions:

1. Preheat oven to 350 degrees F (175 degrees C).
2. Grease a 9x13-inch baking dish.
3. Beat 1 cup white sugar, 1/2 cup butter, and 1 egg in a bowl until smooth.
4. Add sour cream and vanilla extract; mix well.
5. Stir in 3 cups flour, baking soda, and baking powder until mixture comes together in a sticky dough.
6. Spread half the dough evenly into prepared baking dish.
7. Beat cream cheese, 1/2 cup white sugar, and 1 egg in another bowl until smooth.
8. Spoon mixture into baking dish over dough.
9. Drop remaining half of dough by spoonfuls over cream cheese mixture.

10. Mix pecans, brown sugar, 1/3 cup flour, and 1/3 cup butter in a bowl until mixture resembles a coarse crumble; sprinkle over dough.
11. Bake in the preheated oven until a toothpick inserted into the center comes out clean, about 45 minutes.

Polish Noodles and Cottage Cheese

Ingredients:

1/2 cup butter
1 small onion, diced
1 (16 oz.) package egg noodles
1 (16 oz.) package cottage cheese
1/2 cup sour cream
1/2 tsp. sea salt
1/4 tsp. ground black pepper

Directions:

1. Melt butter in a saucepan over medium heat.
2. Cook and stir onion in melted butter until softened, 7 to 10 minutes.
3. Bring a large pot of lightly salted water to a boil.
4. Cook egg noodles in the boiling water, stirring occasionally until cooked through but firm to the bite, about 5 minutes.
5. Drain and return to the pot.
6. Stir butter and onion mixture, cottage cheese, sour cream, sea salt, and black pepper into the noodles.
7. Place the pot over medium heat; cook and stir until heated through and warm, 5 to 8 minutes.

Polish Galicyjskie Cookies

Ingredients:

4 eggs, separated
1/2 cup cream
3 tbsps. confectioners' sugar
1 pinch ground cinnamon
2 3/4 pounds potatoes, peeled, finely grated, and squeezed dry
2 tbsps. raisins (optional)
1 cup all-purpose flour
1 pinch salt
1 cup oil for deep frying confectioners' sugar for dusting

Directions:

1. Beat together the egg yolks, cream 3 tbsps. confectioners' sugar, and cinnamon until smooth.
2. Stir into the grated potatoes along with the raisins, and mix until well combined; then stir in the flour.
3. Beat the egg whites with salt until stiff.
4. Gently fold into the potato mixture.
5. Heat oil to 350 degrees F (175 degrees C) in a deep fryer or electric skillet.
6. Fry the cookies by dropping heaping tbsp.-size dollops into the hot oil.
7. Fry until golden brown on both sides, then drain on a paper towel-lined plate. Dust with confectioners' sugar.

Polish Christmas Cookies

Ingredients:

1 cup butter
1 cup shortening
2 cups white sugar
5 eggs
7 1/2 cups all-purpose flour
6 tsps. baking powder
1/2 tsp. salt
1/2 oz. anise extract

Directions:

1. Preheat oven to 350 degrees F (175 degrees C).
2. Cream the butter, shortening and the sugar together.
3. Stir in the eggs and continue to beat.
4. Add the anise flavoring.
5. Stir in 7 cups of the flour, the baking powder and the salt.
6. Mix until the dough is soft.
7. Add the additional cup of flour if needed. Chill the dough.
8. On a lightly floured surface roll out the dough and cut with cookie cutters.
9. Place cookies on greased cookie sheets.
10. Bake at 350 degrees F (175 degrees C) for 12 to 15 minutes.
11. Frost and decorate when cookies are cooled.

Sweet Polish Cherry Cake

Ingredients:

1 cup white sugar
2 1/2 cups all-purpose flour
1 tbsp. baking powder
1 tsp. baking soda
1 tbsp. butter
2 cups pitted sweet cherries
1 tbsp. white sugar
1/2 cup olive oil
4 eggs
1 (6 oz.) container plain yogurt
1 tbsp. olive oil

Directions:

1. Preheat oven to 350 degrees F (175 degrees C).
2. In a mixing bowl, whisk 1 cup sugar, flour, baking powder, and baking soda together until evenly combined.
3. Melt butter in a skillet over medium heat.
4. Cook and stir the pitted cherries in the butter until they are tender, sprinkling them with 1 tbsp. of sugar, 8 to 10 minutes.
5. Set aside.
6. Form a well in the center of the dry ingredients, and pour in 1/2 cup olive oil, eggs, and yogurt; use your fingers to lightly stir the liquid ingredients into the flour mixture to make a soft dough.
7. Scrape the batter into a 9x12-inch baking dish.
8. Drizzle the batter with 1 tbsp. of olive oil, and top with the cherries.
9. Bake in the preheated oven until the cake is set and golden on top, about 40 minutes.
10. A toothpick inserted into the center of the cake should come out clean.

Polish Yeast Plum Cake - Drozdzowka

Ingredients:
1/2 cup whole milk
1 tbsp. all-purpose flour
1 tbsp. white sugar
2 (0.6 oz.) cakes cake yeast
1 1/3 cups margarine
1/2 cup dry bread crumbs
4 eggs
1 1/8 cups white sugar
8 cups all-purpose flour
4 tsps. vanilla sugar
1 cup whole milk, or as needed
6 cups fresh plums, pitted and quartered
1 1/2 cups all-purpose flour
1/2 cup butter
1/2 cup white sugar
1/2 tsp. ground cinnamon (optional)

Directions:
1. In a saucepan over very low heat, warm up 1/2 cup of milk to no more than 100 degrees F (38 degrees C); stir in 1 tbsp. of flour and 1 tbsp. of sugar.
2. Remove from heat and transfer to a bowl.
3. Crumble the cake yeast into the milk mixture, and gently stir until the mixture becomes creamy.
4. Cover the pan with a cloth, and set aside in a warm place until the yeast forms a spongy texture, 20 to 30 minutes.
5. Melt margarine in a saucepan over low heat; remove from heat and allow to cool to lukewarm.
6. Preheat oven to 350 degrees F (175 degrees C).
7. Grease a 9x13-inch baking dish, and sprinkle with bread crumbs.
8. Place eggs and 1 1/8 cup sugar into a blender, and process until the mixture is yellow and fluffy.

9. In a large mixing bowl, whisk together 8 cups of flour with vanilla sugar.
10. Stir in the egg mixture, activated yeast mixture, and lukewarm margarine; start kneading 1 cup milk, or as needed, into the dough, a little at a time, until the dough stops sticking to your fingers and becomes smooth and even.
11. Knead for at least 15 minutes, working to incorporate as much air as possible into the dough as you knead.
12. Press the dough evenly into the prepared baking sheet, and arrange the plums over the top of the dough.
13. Set aside.
14. In a bowl, cut together 1 1/2 cup flour, the butter, and 1/2 cup of sugar with a pastry cutter until the mixture resembles fine crumbs
15. Sprinkle the streusel mixture over the plums.
16. Dust streusel with cinnamon, if desired.
17. Bake in the preheated oven until a toothpick inserted into the center of the cake comes out clean, 1 hour to 1 hour and 10 minutes.

Polish Apple Pancakes - Racuchy z Jablkami

Ingredients:

2 cups milk
2 cups all-purpose flour
2 eggs
1 tbsp. white sugar
1 tsp. ground cinnamon
1/2 tsp. baking soda
1 pinch salt
2 large apples - peeled, cored, and diced
Vegetable oil, as needed
2 tbsps. confectioners' sugar, or to taste

Directions:

1. Combine milk, flour, eggs, sugar, cinnamon, baking soda, and salt in a large bowl; beat with an electric mixer until smooth and creamy.
2. Mix in apples.
3. Heat 1 tbsp. oil in a skillet over medium-high heat.
4. Drop batter by large spoonfuls into the pan and cook until the edges are dry and the bottom is browned, 3 to 4 minutes.
5. Flip and cook until browned on the other side, 2 to 3 minutes.
6. Repeat with remaining batter.
7. Dust pancakes with confections' sugar.

Polish Stuffed Cabbage

Ingredients:

1 medium head cabbage
water to cover
1 pound ground beef
1 cup cooked rice
garlic powder to taste
1 egg
1 (12 fluid oz.) can tomato juice
1 tbsp. vinegar
1 tbsp. white sugar
Water to cover

Directions:

1. Place the head of cabbage in a large pot over high heat and add water to cover.
2. Boil cabbage for 15 minutes, or until it is pliable and soft.
3. Drain and allow to cool completely.
4. Remove the hard outer vein from the leaves.
5. In a separate large bowl, combine the beef, rice, garlic powder and the egg, mixing well.
6. Place a small amount, about the size of your palm, into the center of a cabbage leaf and fold leaf over, tucking in the sides of the leaf to keep meat mixture inside.
7. Pile up the filled leaves in a large pot, putting the larger leaves on the bottom.
8. Add the tomato juice, vinegar and sugar and enough water to cover.
9. Simmer over medium low heat for about 60 minutes.
10. Keep an eye on them, making sure the bottom of leaves do not burn.)

Bigos - Polish Hunter's Stew

Ingredients:
9 cups boiling water, divided
3 pounds sauerkraut - rinsed, drained and chopped
15 pitted prunes
5 whole allspice berries
3 bay leaves
1 cup dried mushrooms
2 tbsps. vegetable oil
2 onion, chopped
1 Polish sausage, sliced
1/2 pound beef stew meat, cubed
1/2 pound boneless pork shoulder, cubed
1/2 cup bacon strips, diced
1 tbsp. caraway seeds
1 tsp. dried marjoram
salt and pepper to taste
3/4 cup red wine
3 tbsps. tomato paste (Optional)

Directions:
1. Place sauerkraut in a large pan or casserole dish and pour in 4 cups of boiling water.
2. Add prunes, allspice, and bay leaves. Simmer until Sauerkraut is soft, about 50 minutes.
3. Pour about 1 cup of boiling water over mushrooms and soak to rehydrate, about 30 minutes.
4. Drain and chop mushrooms, reserving the liquid.
5. Heat oil in a frying pan over medium to high heat.
6. Add onion and sausage. Sauté while stirring until onion is soft and sausage is browned, about 5 minutes.
7. In a separate pan, bring about 4 cups of water to a boil.
8. Add beef, pork, and bacon. Simmer until cooked through for 20 minutes, then drain.

9. When sauerkraut is soft, add the drained meat mixture, sausage-onion mixture, and soaked mushrooms; mix well. Simmer uncovered over low heat, about 20 minutes.
10. Pour in red wine and cook for 15 minutes until flavors are well blended.
11. Season with caraway seeds, marjoram, salt, and pepper.
12. Stir in tomato puree.
13. If the stew is too dry, pour in some of the water reserved from soaking the mushrooms, and simmer so flavors combine, about 5 minutes.

Chlodnik - Cold Polish Beet Soup

Ingredients:

3 beets with leaves and stems - beets peeled and chopped, leaves sliced
water to cover
1 cup chicken stock
1 small cucumber, grated
1 hard-cooked egg, chopped
⅓ cup chopped fresh dill
3 small green onions, thinly sliced
1 pint buttermilk
1/2 cup sour cream
⅓ lemon, juiced
1/2 tsp. ground black pepper

Directions:

1. Cover beets with water in a pot and bring to a boil; cook until tender about 15 minutes.
2. Remove from heat and stir in chicken stock. Allow beets to cool.
3. Mix cucumber, egg, dill, and green onions in a bowl.
4. Whisk buttermilk and sour cream until smooth in another bowl.
5. Stir egg mixture and buttermilk mixture into cooled beets.
6. Cover and refrigerate at least 2 hours before serving.

Polish Chili

Ingredients:

2 pounds ground beef
1 pound fully cooked Polish sausage or kielbasa, chopped
1 large onion, chopped
3 cloves garlic, minced
4 Anaheim chilies, stemmed, seeded, and chopped
3 yellow wax peppers, seeded and chopped
3 jalapeno peppers, seeded and chopped
4 medium tomatoes, chopped
4 tomatillos, husked and chopped
1/2 cup distilled white vinegar
1/4 cup tomato sauce
1 (4 oz.) jar chopped pimentos, drained
1 (15 oz.) can pinto beans, rinsed and drained
1 (15 oz.) can kidney beans, rinsed and drained

Directions:

1. Place the ground beef into a large pot over medium-high heat.
2. Cook, stirring to crumble, until beef is no longer pink.
3. Drain off excess grease, leaving just enough to coat the bottom of the pot.
4. Add the polish sausage, onion and garlic to the pot; cook and stir until onion is tender.
5. Mix in the Anaheim, yellow and jalapeno peppers, tomatoes and tomatillos.
6. Simmer over medium heat for about 20 minutes.
7. Pour in the vinegar, tomato sauce and pimentos and then mix in the pinto beans and kidney beans.
8. Cover and simmer over medium heat for 30 minutes.

Polish Rice Cake

Ingredients:

2 cups long grain white rice
6 cups skim milk
1 tsp. salt
1 cup butter
1 (8 oz.) package cream cheese
3 eggs
1 cup half-and-half cream
1 tsp. vanilla extract
1 cup self-rising flour
1/2 cup golden raisins

Directions:

1. Combine rice, milk and salt in a saucepan and cook slowly until liquid is absorbed.
2. Stir frequently.
3. Preheat oven to 350 degrees F (175 degrees C).
4. Grease and flour one 9x13 inch baking pan.
5. In large bowl, combine the butter and cream cheese. Cream well with wooden spoon.
6. In another bowl combine eggs, half and half, and vanilla.
7. Add to creamed mixture and blend well.
8. Stir in the cooled rice mixture and mix well.
9. Add the flour and blend well.
10. Stir in the raisins.
11. Pour batter into the prepared pan, pat top to avoid any air bubbles.
12. Bake at 350 degrees F (175 degrees C) for 1 hour.
13. Let cake stand for one hour before turning out of pan.

Polish Jam Crescents - Rogaliki

Ingredients:

3 1/2 oz. compressed fresh yeast
7 tbsps. milk
5 1/2 cups all-purpose flour, or more as needed
2 1/4 cups unsalted butter, at room temperature
4 tbsps. sour cream
4 tbsps. white sugar
2 eggs
3 egg yolks
1 1/2 cups plum jam
2 1/2 cups confectioners' sugar
2 tbsps. water, or as needed

Directions:

1. Stir milk and yeast together in a bowl until smooth.
2. Set aside until foamy, about 10 minutes.
3. Preheat the oven to 350 degrees F (175 degrees C). Line a baking sheet with parchment paper.
4. Combine flour, butter, sour cream, sugar, eggs, and egg yolks in a large bowl.
5. Stir in yeast mixture.
6. Mix well using an electric mixer at first, then using your hands.
7. Turn out dough onto a floured work surface and knead until smooth, adding more flour, 1 tbsp. at a time, if dough is sticking to your hands.
8. Form dough into a long log and cut into 1 1/2-inch rounds.
9. Cover rounds with a cloth.
10. Roll each round of dough into a thin circle.
11. Cut the circle into six triangles, as you would a pizza.
12. Place 1 tsp. jam at the wider end of each triangle, then roll up like a croissant.
13. Place on the prepared baking sheet.
14. Repeat until all the dough is used up.

15. Bake in the preheated oven until rogaliki have risen and are golden brown, about 20 minutes.
16. Remove from oven and cool completely, about 30 minutes.
17. Place confectioners' sugar in a bowl and stir in water, 1 tbsp. at a time, until a drizzling consistency is reached.
18. Drizzle icing over cooled rogaliki.

Polish Babka Cake

Ingredients:

1 1/4 cups all-purpose flour
2 tsps. baking powder
3/4 cup potato starch
3/4 cup unsalted butter, at room temperature
2 tbsps. unsalted butter, at room temperature
1 1/2 cups confectioners' sugar
1 tsp. vanilla sugar
4 eggs, separated
3 tbsps. sour cream, or more to taste
1/2 lemon, zested and juiced
1 tbsp. almond extract
2 tbsps. raisins
1 1/2 tbsps. butter
3 tbsps. dried bread crumbs

Directions:

1. Preheat the oven to 350 degrees F (175 degrees C).
2. Sift all-purpose flour and baking powder into a bowl.
3. Stir in potato starch.
4. Beat 3/4 cup plus 2 tbsps. butter in a bowl using an electric mixer until light and fluffy.
5. Add confectioners' sugar and vanilla sugar; beat until just combined.
6. Add egg yolks and sour cream; mix well.
7. Whisk lemon zest, lemon juice, and almond extract into the batter.
8. Beat egg whites in a glass, metal, or ceramic bowl using clean beaters until stiff peaks form.
9. Beat flour mixture into the batter until no dry spots remain.
10. Gently fold in raisins and egg whites until evenly incorporated.
11. Liberally grease an 8-inch, 6-cup Bundt® cake pan with 1 1/2 tbsps. butter.

12. Sprinkle evenly with bread crumbs. Spoon batter into the prepared pan.
13. Bake in the preheated oven until a toothpick inserted into the center of the cake comes out clean, 30 to 40 minutes.
14. Cool slightly before inverting cake onto a serving plate.

Polish Stewed Cabbage

Ingredients:

2 tbsps. olive oil
2 onions, chopped
1 clove garlic, or more to taste, minced
1 medium head cabbage, cut into squares
1 tsp. white vinegar
1 tsp. caraway seeds
1 tsp. white sugar
1 pound kielbasa sausage, cut into chunks
1 (14.5 oz.) can stewed tomatoes (with garlic and olive oil)
1/4 cup salsa
Salt and ground black pepper to taste

Directions:

1. Heat olive oil in a Dutch oven over medium heat.
2. Cook and stir onions and garlic in hot oil until onion is translucent, 3 to 5 minutes.
3. Stir cabbage, vinegar, caraway seeds, and sugar with the onion mixture; bring to a simmer and cook until the cabbage is softened, about 15 minutes.
4. Stir sausage, tomatoes, and salsa with the cabbage mixture; season with salt and pepper.
5. Place a cover on the Dutch oven and cook until cabbage is completely tender, 45 to 60 minutes.

Polish Perogies

Ingredients:

4 1/2 cups all-purpose flour
2 tsps. salt
2 tbsps. butter, melted
2 cups sour cream
2 eggs
1 egg yolk
2 tbsps. vegetable oil
8 baking potatoes, peeled and cubed
1 cup shredded Cheddar cheese
2 tbsps. processed cheese sauce
1 dash onion salt to taste
Salt and pepper to taste

Directions:

1. In a large bowl, stir together the flour and salt.
2. In a separate bowl, whisk together the butter, sour cream, eggs, egg yolk and oil.
3. Stir the wet ingredients into the flour until well blended.
4. Cover the bowl with a towel, and let stand for 15 to 20 minutes.
5. Place potatoes into a pot, and fill with enough water to cover.
6. Bring to a boil, and cook until tender, about 15 minutes.
7. Drain, and mash with shredded cheese and cheese sauce while still hot.
8. Season with onion salt, salt and pepper.
9. Set aside to cool.
10. Separate the perogie dough into two balls.
11. Roll out one piece at a time on a lightly floured surface until it is thin enough to work with, but not too thin so that it tears.
12. Cut into circles using a cookie cutter, perogie cutter, or a glass.

13. Brush a little water around the edges of the circles, and spoon some filling into the center.
14. Fold the circles over into half-circles, and press to seal the edges.
15. Place perogies on a cookie sheet, and freeze.
16. Once frozen, transfer to freezer storage bags or containers.
17. To cook perogies:
18. Bring a large pot of lightly salted water to a boil.
19. Drop perogies in one at a time.
20. They are done when they float to the top.
21. Do not boil too long, or they will be soggy!
22. Remove with a slotted spoon.

About the Author

Laura Sommers is **The Recipe Lady!**

She lives on a small farm in Baltimore County, Maryland and has a passion for all things domestic especially when it comes to saving money. She has a profitable eBay business and is a couponing addict. Follow her tips and tricks to learn how to make delicious meals on a budget, save money or to learn the latest life hack!

Follow her on Pinterest:

http://pinterest.com/therecipelady1

Visit the Recipe Lady's blog for even more great recipes:

http://the-recipe-lady.blogspot.com/

Visit her Amazon Author Page to see her latest books:

amazon.com/author/laurasommers

Follow the Recipe Lady on Facebook:

https://www.facebook.com/therecipegirl

Follow her on Twitter:

https://twitter.com/TheRecipeLady1

Other Books by Laura Sommers

- German Christmas Cookbook
- Christmas Hot Chocolate Recipes
- Christmas Fruitcake Recipes
- Christmas Cookies
- Christmas Pie Cookbook
- Christmas Eggnog Cookbook
- Christmas Coffee Cookbook
- Christmas Candy Cane Cookbook
- Christmas Gingerbread Recipes
- Christmas Stuffing Recipes

Made in the USA
Monee, IL
13 December 2021